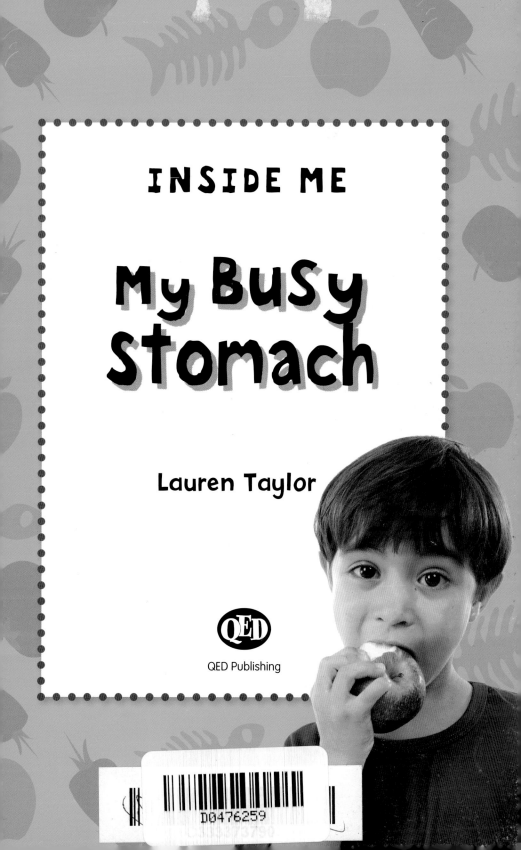

INSIDE ME

My Busy Stomach

Lauren Taylor

QED

QED Publishing

Copyright © QED Publishing 2013

First published in the UK
in 2013 by
QED Publishing
A Quarto Group Company
230 City Road,
London EC1V 2TT

www.qed-publishing.co.uk

A catalogue record for this book is
available from the British Library.

ISBN 978 1 78171 219 1

Printed in China

Consultant Jillian Harker and
Mary Lindeen
Editor Alexandra Koken
Designer Melissa Alaverdy

Picture credits
(t=top, b=bottom, l=left, r=right,
c=center, fc=front cover)
Getty: 19 Tim Hall
Shutterstock: 1 Vinicius Tupinamba,
5 Martin Allinger, 7, 8 Olga
Lyubkina, 9 Mikhail hoboton Popov,
10 Ryan McVal, 11 Jaimie Duplass,
12-13 Sergiy, 15 Blaj Gabriel, 16
Marcus VDT, 17 Olga Lyubkina,
18 Yury Imaging, 21 MarFot, 22l
Lyudmilla Suvorova, 22b Elena
Itsenko, 22t majaan, 23 Brian
Wancho

Words in **bold**
can be found in
the Glossary on
page 24.

Contents

What is your digestive system?

You eat food. The food moves through your body. It goes through your **digestive system.**

Your body uses what it needs.

It gets rid of what it does not need.

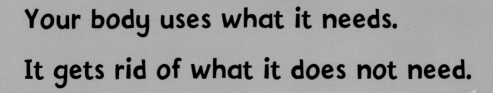

Food

Food keeps your body warm.

It keeps you well.

Fish, meat, eggs and nuts help you grow. They help you get better if you get hurt.

Bread, cereal and pasta give you energy.

More food!

Milk, cheese and butter make strong bones.

Fruits and vegetables have **vitamins**. They have **minerals** too. Your body needs these **nutrients**.

Your body needs water too. Drinking water helps keeps you healthy.

Mouth

Your teeth and tongue help you eat. Your front teeth are for biting.

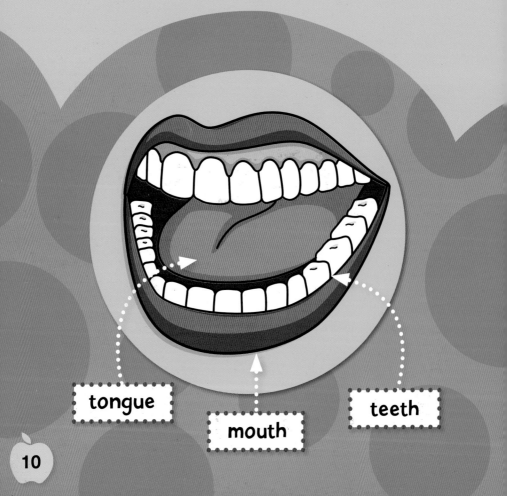

tongue

mouth

teeth

Your back teeth
are for chewing.
Your tongue helps
you swallow.

Oesophagus

Chewed-up food goes down a tube in your neck.

This tube is called the **oesophagus** (a-sof-a-gus).

oesophagus

Stomach

Your oesophagus pushes food down. It pushes the food into your stomach.

oesophagus

stomach

Food stays there for about 3 hours. It is turned into tiny pieces. It is digested.

Small intestine

Next, food goes through your small **intestine**. This takes about 4 hours.

Here the food gets very watery. It gets very runny. Nutrients from the food go into your blood.

oesophagus

stomach

small intestine

Liver and blood

The blood goes to your **liver**. Your liver makes a special juice. It is called **bile**.

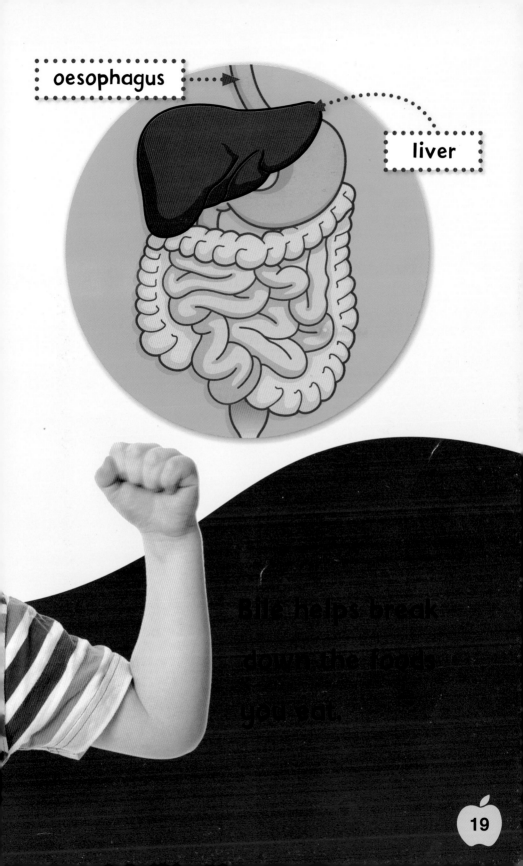

oesophagus

liver

Bile helps break down the foods you eat.

19

Large intestine

What is left of your food goes to the large intestine. What is left is waste. Your body does not need it.

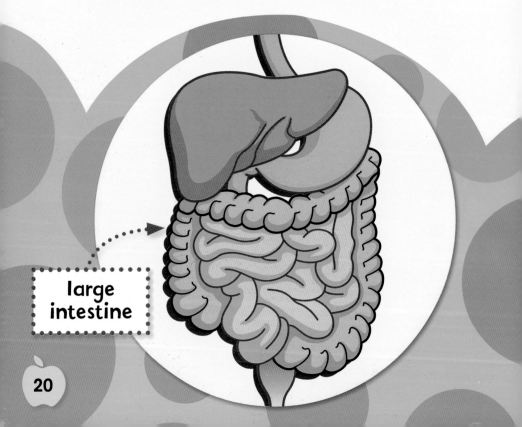

large intestine

Waste is pushed out of your body. It comes out through an opening in your bottom.

Healthy digestive system

You can keep your digestive system healthy. Eat foods such as fruit and wholegrain bread.

Drink lots of water.
Your body will
thank you!

Glossary

bile   a green liquid made by the liver
              that helps digest food

digestive the parts of the body used
system   to break down food so that it can
              be absorbed into the blood

intestine a long tube below the stomach
              that digests food and absorbs liquids

liver   the part of the body that makes bile
              and cleans the blood

minerals one of the things in food that
              bodies need to stay healthy

nutrients minerals, vitamins or any other
              substance people need to eat in
              order to stay healthy

oesophagus the tube that carries food from
              the throat to the stomach

vitamins one of the things in food that
              bodies need to stay healthy